All Me, All the Time

THE AUTHORIZED ART-O-BIOGRAPHY OF

_____

Written by _____ and Karla Oceanak

Illustrated by _____ and Kendra Spanjer

This book was written, drawn, and otherwise
brilliantly created in the year _____ in the
city of _____ in the home
of the _____ family on the
street called _____.

COOL!
I CAN'T WAIT
TO READ IT!

BAILIWICK PRESS

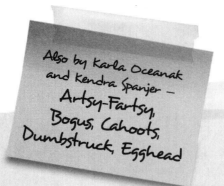

Also by Karla Oceanak
and Kendra Spanjer —
Artsy-Fartsy,
Bogus, Cahoots,
Dumbstruck, Egghead

All Me, All the Time is part of the Aldo Zelnick Comic Novel Series.

Copyright © 2012 by Karla Oceanak and Kendra Spanjer

Published by:
Bailiwick Press
309 East Mulberry Street
Fort Collins, Colorado 80524
(970) 672-4878
Fax: (970) 672-4731
www.bailiwickpress.com
www.aldozelnick.com

Manufactured by:
Friesens Corporation, Altona, Canada
April 2012
Job # 74852

Book cover design by:
Launie Parry
Red Letter Creative
www.red-letter-creative.com

ISBN 978-1-934649-20-6

Library of Congress Control Number: 2012907008

21 20 19 18 17 16 15 14 13 12   7 6 5 4 3 2 1

Dear fellow kid—

If you ever wanted to write a book about the person you know best, here's your chance. Fill in the blanks in this book and *bam!*—instant classic on your family's bookshelf. (Hint: Write at least a couple nice things about your parents. They might raise your allowance.)

But this book's not just for writing. It's also for drawing. That's why it's called an art-o-biography instead of a plain old autobiography.

My name is Aldo Zelnick, by the way, and I make art-o-biographies too. (Check 'em out sometime. People tell me they're funny.)

So what are you waiting for? You've got a whole book to create!

Aldo Zelnick

p.s. Ask a grown-up to take a picture of you holding your finished art-o-biography and post it on the Aldo Zelnick Facebook page!

MEET MY MENTORS:

I'm Goosy—Aldo's grandma. Some people think they're not artistic, and in case you're one of them, I wanted to tell you Pffff! Everyone's at least a _little bit_ artsy-fartsy! So draw away! Just be creative and have fun with it.

Mr. Mot is my name, and words are my game. I'm Aldo's neighbor and a retired English teacher. I've embellished this book with writing pointers—nay, _encouragement!_—for you are now an author. Write well and often.

OH, AND ONE MORE THING...

HOW TO COOLIFY YOUR COVER

THIS IS <u>YOUR</u> ART-O-BIOGRAPHY, SO IT <u>HAS</u> TO HAVE YOUR FACE ON THE FRONT, RIGHT?!

WRITE YOUR NAME BIG AND BODACIOUS HERE, AND DRAW OR PASTE A PHOTO OF YOURSELF HERE. THEN FILL UP THE REST OF THE COVER, FRONT AND BACK, WITH STUFF YOU LOVE. TAPE OR GLUE PICTURES, KEEPSAKES, CANDY WRAPPERS, STICKERS—ANYTHING THAT HELPS TELL THE STORY OF YOU. DON'T FORGET TO DOODLE! YOU CAN EVEN DECORATE THE BORING WHITE INSIDE COVERS HOWEVER YOU WANT.

LIKE GOOSY SAYS, JUST BE CREATIVE AND HAVE FUN WITH IT!

THIS IS ME

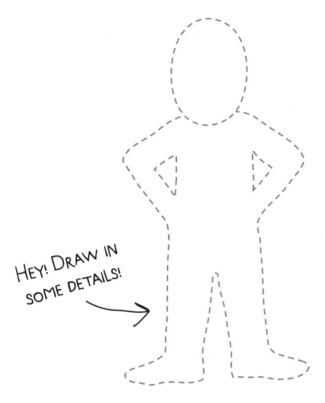

HEY! DRAW IN SOME DETAILS!

I was born on the _____ day of the month of

_____ in the year _____.

That makes me _____ years old now.

When I was born, I was _____ inches long

and weighed _____ pounds and _____ ounces. Now

I'm _____ feet, _____ inches tall and weigh about

_____ pounds. As you can see, I've got a remarkable

talent for growing.

My hair color is _____.

It's more or less the color of _____.

(I YANKED A COUPLE PIECES OF HAIR FROM MY HEAD AND TAPED THEM HERE TO PROVE IT.) →

My hair is (circle all that apply):

STRAIGHT   WAVY   CURLY   LONG   SHORT   MEDIUM

My eyes are _____. They're the color of

_____.

There. Now you have a description of me in case I decide to run away and you are heartbroken (which you naturally would be) and want help finding me.

Specify!
The more detailed and specific your words, the better your readers can imagine your story. For example, if your eyes are blue, maybe they're the color of faded blue jeans!

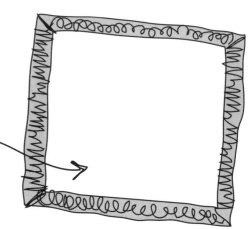

(BTW, if I were going to run away, here's where I'd

go: _____. Just so you know.)

FOR THOSE OF YOU WHO'VE NEVER HAD THE PRIVILEGE OF MEETING ME...

First of all, I'm sorry.

Second of all, I'm going to write down some stuff so you won't feel so left out.

People say I'm _____ and

_____.

Inside of me, I know I'm _____ and

_____.

Here's a short, true story about me that lets you

know what I'm like. One day: _____

_____

_____

_____

_____

_____

_____.

RANSOM-NOTE NAME

I cut out letters from a magazine and pasted them here so you can see what my first, middle, and last names would look like in a ransom note.

Get edgy! When you're working with paper to create a piece of art, try tearing the edges instead of cutting with scissors.

YOUR FACE

Now, look in a mirror and, as you make each expression, draw how it looks!

PLAIN

MEGA-HAPPY

SUPER-ANGRY

UBER-SAD

BEGGING/PLEADING

REALLY. REALLY. BORED.

PAUSE FOR A VERY IMPORTANT TEST

Can you wiggle your ears?   yes   no

Can you raise just one eyebrow?   yes   no

Can you roll your tongue?   yes   no

Can you whistle?   yes   no

Can you touch your nose with your tongue?   yes   no

Do your eyebrows meet in the middle?   yes   no

Do you have any boogers showing right now?   yes   no

How many freckles do you have on your face?

   0   10-25   26-50   51-100   100+

Is your face perfectly symmetrical? Look closely.
What's different between the two sides of your face?

_____

_____

How many ducks could a duck duct-tape, if a duck could duct-tape ducks?

There was a minimum of cinnamon in the aluminum pan.

MY TALENTS

I'm good at certain things. Such as:

- _____

- _____

I'm not so good at other things. Like:

- _____

- _____

FIRSTS

First thing I remember from when I was little:

_____

_____

First place I ever lived:

_____

First best friend:

_____

First teacher:

_____

First airplane ride or big trip:

_____

_____

First kiss:
(Hang on...you've already had your first kiss?!)

_____

First cousins:

_____   _____

_____   _____

First thing I remember getting in big trouble for:
(Gimme details!)

_____

_____

First Halloween costume I remember:

_____

_____

(I drew it here so you can see how awesome I looked.)

DID YOU NOTICE THAT WHEN YOU SAY THE WORD "FIRST" OVER AND OVER AGAIN, IT STARTS TO SOUND LIKE NONSENSE?

Trying new food is fun! You might be surprised by what "grows on you"! [Get it??]

Rate-A-Veggie
Pictures by Bee
Ratings by you

Asparagus
☆☆☆☆☆

Broccoli
☆☆☆☆☆

Beets
☆☆☆☆☆

Brussels sprouts
☆☆☆☆☆

Bell peppers
☆☆☆☆☆

Carrots
☆☆☆☆☆

Cauliflower

☆☆☆☆☆

Mushrooms

(ok, really a fungus, but...)

☆☆☆☆☆☆

Corn

☆☆☆☆☆☆

Onions

☆☆☆☆☆☆

Eggplant

☆☆☆☆☆

Peas

☆☆☆☆☆☆

Lettuce

☆☆☆☆☆☆

Radishes

☆☆☆☆☆☆

Zucchini

☆☆☆☆☆☆

MY FAVORITES

Cereal: _____

MEAL:

Fruit: _____

Dessert: _____

Candy: _____

Gum: _____

BEVERAGE:

Pop: _____

Restaurant: _____

ICE CREAM FLAVOR:

Holiday: _____

Season: _____

Number: _____

Day of the week: _____

TIME OF DAY:

Movie: _____

Actor: _____

TV show: _____

BOOK:

COMIC CHARACTER:

Board game
or card game:

_____

Song or type of music:

_____

TOY:

Video game: _____

School subject: _____

Dinosaur: _____

ANIMAL:

Bird: _____

Bug: _____

MY BEST LOOK

FAVORITE
HEADWEAR

FAVORITE OUTFIT
(HEY BOYS: THIS
MEANS "CLOTHES")

FAVORITE
FOOTWEAR

ART BREAK: DRAW IT 4 TIMES

Pick a small object and draw it in box #1 large enough to fill the space. Then draw the object 3 more times, making it better and better each time.

#1

#2

#3

#4

ME-O-METER

How tidy I keep my room:

How bad I am at getting up early:

How faithful I am at brushing my teeth twice a day:

How finicky an eater I am:

How nice I am to my siblings:

How carefully I do my homework:

How much I like school:

How much I like to read:

How much I like to draw:

How much I like to write:

How big of a tantrum I throw sometimes:

ITZA PIZZA FANTASTICA

I've topped my pizza with my favorite things and colored everything in. I drew an arrow to the slice(s) reserved for me.

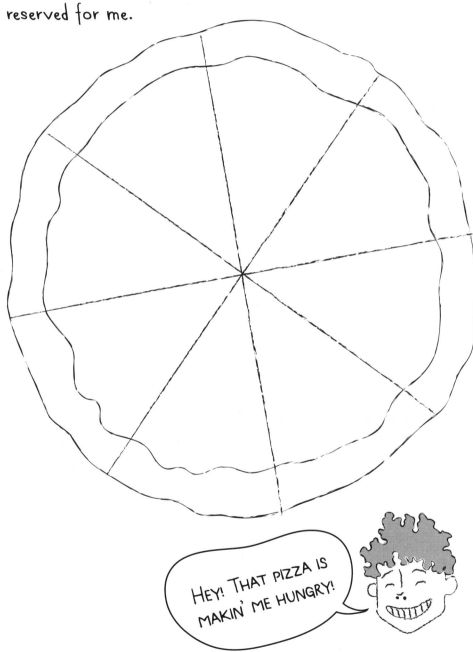

SCAREDY-PANTS

I'm a little bit afraid of _____,

and _____.

Things that <u>really</u> scare the bejeebers out of me are

_____ and

_____.

Art break!
Use the grid lines to finish this drawing with its mirror half.
(Hint: turn your journal upside-down, forget about the alien, and just draw the lines you see!)

Here's a story about the scariest thing that's ever happened to me: _____

_____

_____

_____

_____

_____

_____

_____

Double-stuff!
Strong stories have a beginning, a middle, and an end. Make your story like an Oreo cookie—full of good stuff in the middle.

_____

_____

_____

_____

_____

_____

BODACIOUS BOOKS

Here are some of the books I've read and liked:

_____ _____

_____ _____

_____ _____

_____ _____

I really like books that _____

_____

_____.

I really don't like books that _____

_____

_____.

If I could live in a world from one book I've read,

I'd pick _____ because

_____

_____.

If I could pick one character to come live with me in the real world with me, I'd pick: _____

_____

because _____

_____

_____.

HERE'S A PICTURE OF US HANGING OUT.

WHAT IFS

If I'm ever crazy enough to get a tattoo, it would

be of a _____

and look something like →

I'd put it on my:

_____

If I could get out
of doing one thing for
the rest of my life, I'd pick:

_____

because _____

_____.

If I could eat junk food at every meal, I'd eat:

_____ for breakfast,

_____ for lunch, and

_____ for dinner.

(Wait. Now what would be the point of dessert?!)

If I could give just <u>one person</u> one very special gift—
anything I wanted to give them—I'd choose this person:

_____

and I would give them _____

_____.

If I ever colored my hair a different color, I'd color it:

_____.

If I could have one super-power, I'd choose:

_____

because _____

_____.

If I could pick one thing to grow on trees (other
than money), I'd pick: _____

_____.

If I could do anything I wanted to for one day, no matter how much it cost or whether my parents said OK, my day would go something like this:

_____

_____

_____

_____

_____

_____

_____

_____

Next!
Don't forget to use transition words to help move us through your day: first, then, next, after, later, meanwhile, soon, finally...

_____

_____

_____

_____

GIVE MYSELF A HAND

This is a pencil tracing of my hand. I've drawn my knuckles, fingernails, scars, rings, etc., and I've colored everything in so you can see what color my skin is.

Oh, by the way, I'm ☐ LEFT ☐ RIGHT -handed.

COLOR YOUR <u>ACTUAL</u> FINGERTIPS WITH <u>WASHABLE</u> MARKER AND PRESS SOME FINGERPRINTS AROUND THE EDGES OF THIS PAGE TO PROVE IT'S YOU!

MY SCHEDULE

To give my future biographers a headstart, I wrote out what I do every day. I put a green circle around the best parts, and a red box around the worst parts.

<u>School Days</u>	<u>My Days Off</u>
7:00 A.M.	7:00 A.M.
8:00	8:00
9:00	9:00
10:00	10:00
11:00	11:00
12:00 P.M.	12:00 P.M.
1:00	1:00
2:00	2:00
3:00	3:00
4:00	4:00
5:00	5:00
6:00	6:00
7:00	7:00
8:00	8:00
9:00	9:00
10:00	10:00

ART BREAK: COLOR WHEEL

These things are so handy! Color this one and fill in the blanks for each of the three secondary colors.

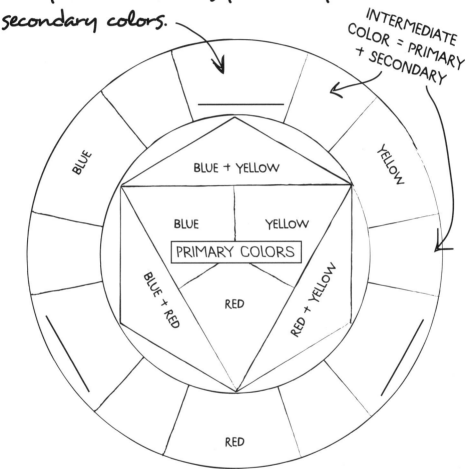

INTERMEDIATE COLOR = PRIMARY + SECONDARY

BLUE

YELLOW

BLUE + YELLOW

BLUE | YELLOW

PRIMARY COLORS

BLUE + RED

RED

RED + YELLOW

RED

Complementary colors (pairs that make each other look brighter) are directly across from each other on the color wheel. They are:

RED & _____, BLUE & _____,

and YELLOW & _____.

MY FAMILY

Name: _____

Relationship to me: _____

Age: _____

Fun fact: _____

Responsibilities: _____

Name: _____

Relationship to me: _____

Age: _____

Fun fact: _____

Responsibilities: _____

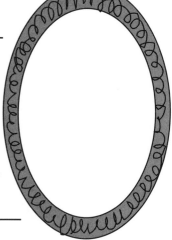

Name: _____

Relationship to me: _____

Age: _____

Fun fact: _____

Responsibilities: _____

Name: _____

Relationship to me: _____

Age: _____

Fun fact: _____

Responsibilities: _____

Name: _____

Relationship to me: _____

Age: _____

Fun fact: _____

Responsibilities: _____

Name: _____

Relationship to me: _____

Age: _____

Fun fact: _____

Responsibilities: _____

MY PETS

Can't forget about them!

Name: _____

Type: _____

Description: _____

_____

Favorite treat: _____

Name: _____

Type: _____

Description: _____

_____

Favorite treat: _____

Name: _____

Type: _____

Description: _____

_____

Favorite treat: _____

MY PET PEEVES
(JUST THE TOP 10)

So, thinking about my pets led me to thinking about my pet peeves, which are the things that really bother me.

10. _____

9. _____

8. _____

7. _____

6. _____

5. _____

4. _____

3. _____

2. _____

... and the thing that bugs me the very most is...

1. _____

_____

WHAT IT'S LIKE TO BE A

_____
MY LAST NAME

My family likes to _____ and

_____.

I guess you could say we're _____

_____.

We live in a _____ that has

_____ and _____.

It doesn't have _____.

We're different from other families in these ways:

1. _____

2. _____

3. _____

4. _____

What I love about my family is _____

_____.

Sometimes I wish my family could _____

_____.

At my house, it's never OK to _____

_____.

When I _____

_____, my parents go ballistic.

If you break the rules at my house, here's what

happens: _____

_____

_____

_____

_____

My favorite holiday is _____,

when we usually _____

_____.

My favorite holiday memory is _____

_____

_____.

If you were a giant who could quietly lift off the roof of my house without anyone noticing, here's what you'd probably see each of us doing inside:

_____

_____

_____

_____

_____

_____

_____.

YE OLDE FAMILY CREST

Here's a cool-looking crest I just made up! In each of the 4 quadrants is a picture of something that is important to us and defines us as a family. I colored it, added some patterns and wrote our last name at the bottom in my best handwriting. Authentic, isn't it?

SNACK BREAK!

I matched up the snacks I'd pick for each snack-ortunity.

POTATO CHIPS

HUMMUS

BEEF JERKY

ICE CREAM

TAQUITO

APPLE

M&Ms

SNICKERDOODLE

(OR OTHER COOKIE OF YOUR CHOICE)

CARROTS

POPCORN

SLUSHIE

NUTS

SALSA & TORTILLA CHIPS

AFTER SCHOOL

RECESS

FORT TIME

SECOND BREAKFAST

LATE NIGHT

COUCH POTATO TIME

FUN IN THE SUN

MOVIE THEATER

NEVER

CAMPING

SPORT ACTIVITY

SATURDAY AFTERNOON

NEVER EVER

UH, I PICK TAQUITO. FOR EVERY SNACK.

ART BREAK: "BLIND" CONTOUR DRAWING

Get someone to sit still while you look at them closely and draw what you see. But there's a catch! Two, actually: 1. You can't lift your pencil once you start drawing, and 2. you're NOT allowed to look at your paper!

No peeking! How accurate can you be with one crazy, wiggly line? For extra fun, have your model do a "blind" contour drawing of you at the same time!

SUPERHERO-MATIC

As soon as I realized that some cartoonists are rich and famous, I decided to become one. I started by creating my own superhero character, Bacon Boy!

Bacon is my favorite food, so that was a natural choice. I even gave him a sidekick—his dog, C.W. (It stands for Cocktail Weenie.)

Then I cooked up an easy, 3-step way for other kids to create their very own superfood-hero! Give it a try!

If you already have a comic book character, you can draw him/her here. (BTW, you can use the superhero-matic to generate sidekicks and supervillains, too.)

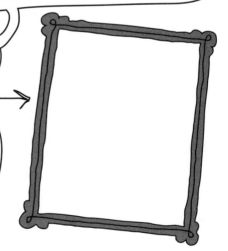

STEP 1

THINK UP 6 FOODS. WRITE ONE FOOD ON EACH LINE, THEN GIVE YOURSELF 1 MINUTE TO DRAW AS MANY LITTLE SKETCHES OF THAT FOOD IN ITS BOX AS YOU CAN. IN 6 MINUTES YOU'LL HAVE 6 BOXES FULL OF IDEAS.

_____   _____

_____   _____

_____   _____

STEP 2

LIST AS MANY SUPER POWERS OR HERO-TYPE GADGETS AS YOU CAN POSSIBLY THINK OF. THEY CAN BE FROM OTHER COMICS OR MOVIES YOU LIKE, OR THEY CAN BE 100% MADE-UP.

_____   _____

_____   _____

_____   _____

_____   _____

_____   _____

_____   _____

_____   _____

_____   _____

Is the superhero you're creating going to be (circle one):

GOOD?   EVIL?

STEP 3

ALMOST DONE! GO BACK TO STEP 1 AND CHOOSE YOUR FAVORITE FOOD DRAWING. DRAW IT BIGGER IN THE BOX BELOW—ADDING EYES, ARMS, WINGS, TAILS, ETC.

NOW LOOK AT STEP 2 AND CHOOSE THE BEST COUPLE OF POWERS. DRAW THE POWERS ON AND AROUND YOUR CHARACTER AND, IF YOU WANT, ADD A CAPE, A BIG LETTER ON THE CHEST, A STEED, AND ANY OTHER SUPER-GEAR YOU LIKE. COLOR EVERYTHING.

Finally, give him or her a super-awesome name:

TA-DA!

WHERE I LIVE

Here's how the outside of my house/apartment looks:

It's on a street with _____

_____.

Other places near my house are _____

and _____.

My neighborhood is kinda _____.

I've lived here for _____ years. This is the (circle one):

FIRST   SECOND   THIRD   FOURTH   FIFTH   place I've lived.

MY ROOM

☐ I have my own room.

☐ I have to share a room with _____.

Favorite things about my room:

_____

_____

_____

Worst things about my room:

_____

_____

_____

Three things I wish I could have in my room that I don't:

1. _____

2. _____

3. _____

MY ACTUAL ROOM

Here's the layout of my room from a bird's-eye point of view, including where the doors and windows are, and where all my furniture and stuff goes.

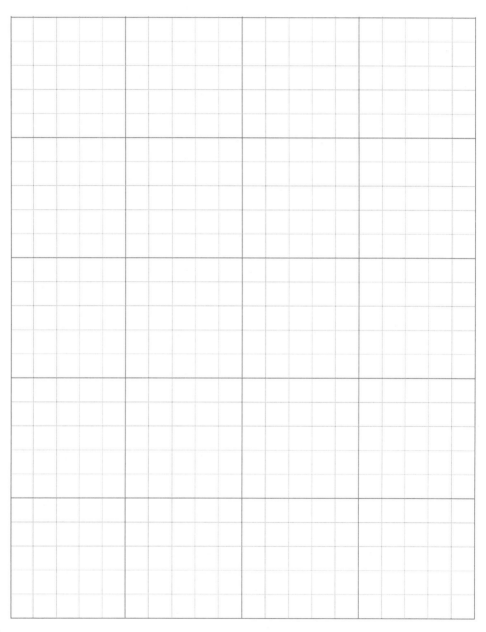

MY FANTASY ROOM

...And this is how my my ideal room and room-stuff would look if I could make them exactly the way I want them.

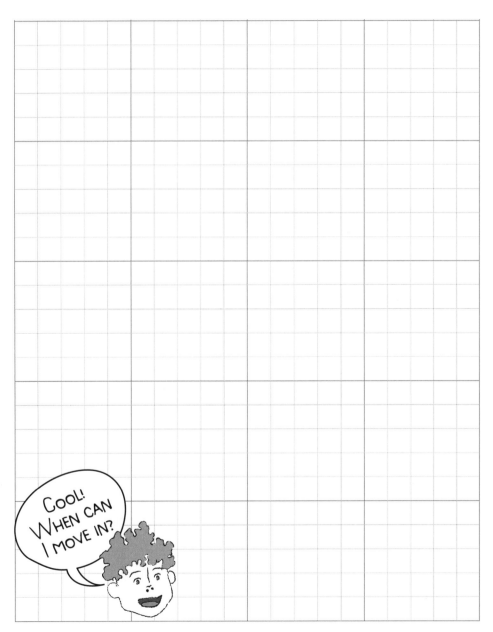

UNDER MY BED

Here's all the stuff that's under or stuck behind my bed right now:

_____   _____

_____   _____

_____   _____

_____   _____

_____   _____

I drew some of it also:

THE CRAZIEST THINGS I'VE EVER FOUND UNDER MY BED? A NEARLY-FULL BOX OF PETRIFIED FRENCH FRIES, A SOCK FROM WHEN I WAS THE SIZE OF A CHIHUAHUA, AND MY BROTHER'S IPOD.

HOW'D THAT GET THERE!?

THE PERFECT FORT

A fort is a place just for kids, where we can go to chillax and get away from it all.

If I could make a fort anywhere and anyhow I wanted, here's what it would look like:

And here's a short list of things I would have in it:

_____   _____

_____   _____

_____   _____

_____   _____

_____   _____

MY TOWN

I live in _____,

which is in the state/province of _____

and the country called _____.

The best thing about my town is _____

_____.

The worst thing about my town is _____

_____.

If I wrote a letter to an alien telling him what to expect when he landed in my town, here's what I'd say:

Dear Alien,

_____

_____

_____

_____

_____

Live long and prosper, _____

WHERE ELSE I'VE BEEN

I've colored in all the U.S. states that have had the privilege of feeling my footsteps. (You might want to turn this baby sideways to get the full effect.)

POOR ALASKA ALWAYS LOOKS SO SMALL ON U.S. MAPS.

WORLD TRAVELER

On these pages I've drawn an X on any country I've visited or lived in, a ☆ on everywhere I hope to go someday, and then I colored <u>everything</u> so none of the countries would feel left out.

Color it crazy!

MY FRIENDS (GIRLS CALL THEM BFFs)

Name: _____

Friends since: _____

Fun fact: _____

We like to: _____

_____

Name: _____

Friends since: _____

Fun fact: _____

We like to: _____

_____

Name: _____

Friends since: _____

Fun fact: _____

We like to: _____

_____

YUP, WE GO WAY BACK

Here's a true story about a time when a friend and I did something really awesome:

_____

_____

_____

_____

_____.

And here's a story about a time when a friend and I got into trouble or had a not-fun time:

_____

_____

Pow!
Choose zingy verbs to make your stories more exciting. Instead of saying "went," try "tippy-toed" or "hustled."

_____

_____

_____

_____

_____.

LINGO

Code words or silly things
other kids and I say: ...which means:

_____   _____

_____   _____

_____   _____

_____   _____

Words my family uses: ...which means:

_____   _____

_____   _____

_____   _____

_____   _____

Here are a few words that tickle my tongue
tantalizingly when I say them:

_____ _____ _____

_____ _____ _____

_____ _____ _____

WORD CLOUD

I've thought of 10 words that represent my dream life and written them here:

SCHOOLED

The name of my school is _____.

I'm in (or will be going into) _____ grade.

Here are some unique things that you might not know about my school:

_____

_____

_____

_____

If I was in charge of my school, I would:

_____

_____

_____

_____

_____

_____

My school mascot is:

_____

My favorite subjects: My unfavorite subjects:

_____   _____

_____   _____

_____   _____

My favorite school lunch is _____.

My unfavoritest school lunch is _____.

At recess I like to: _____

_____.

Show me! Draw your favorite thing about art class!

My teacher's name is _____.

She/he is pretty: _____

_____.

Other teachers I've had:

GRADE	TEACHER NAME	RATING
_____	_____	☆☆☆☆☆
_____	_____	☆☆☆☆☆
_____	_____	☆☆☆☆☆
_____	_____	☆☆☆☆☆
_____	_____	☆☆☆☆☆

The best teacher I've ever had and why: _____

_____

_____

The worst teacher I've ever had and why: _____

_____

_____

WONDERS & WORRIES

Things I wonder about:

_____

_____

_____

_____

_____

I WONDER ABOUT WHEN FLYING CARS WILL BE INVENTED AND WHY CANDY DOESN'T ALWAYS COME IN MOVIE-SIZE BOXES.

I WORRY ABOUT GETTING BAD GRADES AND RUNNING OUT OF BACON.

_____

_____

_____

_____

Things I worry about:

Rate-A-Sport
Pictures by Bee
Ratings by you

Climbing trees might be my favorite sport, but I like lots of others. How about you?

Football
☆☆☆☆☆

Baseball
☆☆☆☆☆

Soccer
☆☆☆☆☆

Volleyball
☆☆☆☆☆

Lacrosse
☆☆☆☆☆

Tennis
☆☆☆☆☆

Frisbee

☆☆☆☆☆

Skateboarding

☆☆☆☆☆

Kickball

☆☆☆☆☆

Swimming

☆☆☆☆☆

Basketball

☆☆☆☆☆

Golf

☆☆☆☆☆

Bicycling

☆☆☆☆☆

Bowling

☆☆☆☆☆

Ping pong

☆☆☆☆☆

THIS IS MY BRAIN

Here's a diagram that shows the things I'm thinking about most of the time.

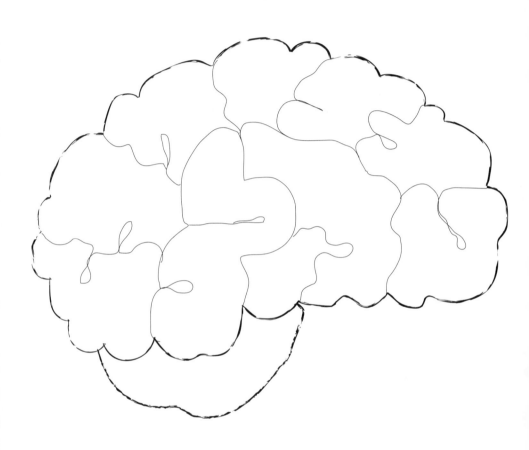

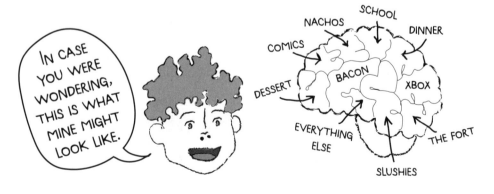

WRITER'S BLOCK: DIALOGUE

Dialogue is what it's called when characters say something in a book or a movie. Write an imaginary dialogue between you and your best friend. Pretend that you want to watch a movie and your friend wants to go for a bike ride. Try to make the dialogue sound real—what each of you would actually say.

YOU:

FRIEND:

YOU:

FRIEND:

YOU:

FRIEND:

YOU:

YOU GET THE LAST WORD!

MY BUCKET

Here are some of the things I want to make sure I do while I'm still a kid.

(Ack! That's only _____ more years!)

_____

_____

_____

_____

_____

_____

_____

_____

TREE FORT
TIME MACHINE

If I could crawl into my fort and magically go anywhere I wanted, to any time in the past, present, or future, I'd go to:

_____

in the year _____

so I could _____

_____.

While I'm there, I'd probably _____

and _____.

I'd take _____ with me.

I'd probably stay there for about _____

DAYS / WEEKS / MONTHS / YEARS. (circle one)

And just so you wouldn't miss me too much while I was gone, I'd make sure _____

_____.

TO HIGHER SCHOOLS...
AND BEYOND!

In high school, I'm probably gonna _____

_____.

I'll still be friends with _____ and

_____, and I'll pick them up in my

car so we can go to _____ on

Saturday nights. All the teachers will know me as the

kid who _____.

I might even set a school record for _____

_____.

After high school, I think I'll _____

_____

_____.

I want to do this because _____

_____

_____.

I'll need to learn more about _____,

so I'll _____.

When I'm living in my very first apartment, away

from my mom and dad, I'll eat _____

for breakfast and _____ for dinner.

I'll never _____ or

_____, and I'll always

_____ and _____.

I'll probably live about _____ miles away from

my family. But I'll go visit them _____ times every

DAY / WEEK / MONTH / YEAR. (circle one)

When I move out on my own, I'll take _____

with me. But I won't take _____.

No way.

WHEN I'M PRESIDENT

The first bill I will push through Congress and sign

into law will be _____

_____.

I will outlaw _____

_____.

I will make an amendment to the Constitution that says

_____

_____.

Everyone will love me so much they'll put bumper

stickers on their car that say:

" _____ "

For my Vice President, I'll pick _____.

I'll have _____

installed in every room of the White House.

I might even have the White House painted my favorite color, so it will be called the _____ House. I'll make _____ a national holiday. I'll make it fashionable to wear _____ and _____ to important dinners. And speaking of dinner, the _____ House chef will make me _____ and _____ whenever I want them.

OK, so maybe there are a few serious world problems I'll solve too, like _____ and _____. For the rest of history, I'll be forever remembered as the President who

_____

_____

_____

_____

EXCUSE ME, MR./MS. PRESIDENT. HOW DOES NATIONAL BACON DAY GRAB YA?

HOW IT'S GONNA BE

When I grow up, I'm going to learn how to _____

_____

so I can be a _____.

My family is going to consist of _____

_____ and _____

and maybe _____.

I'm going to live in _____,

so that I'm close to _____ and

_____.

My house will be _____

_____ and will have

_____.

I'm going to drive a _____and spend

my free time _____

_____.

I'll probably make about $_____ each week, and I'll spend it on _____,

_____, and _____.

Mostly, my life will be _____

_____.

And my parents? I hope that they _____

_____

_____.

THIS IS A PICTURE OF FUTURE-ME. DON'T I LOOK GREAT?

ART BREAK: STRONG VALUES

Using only a pen or a pencil, you can add shadows, 3D-ness, and the suggestion of dark and light colors to your drawings. Just follow my lead!

DARK ——————————————— LIGHT

Stippling

Your turn:

Hatching

Your turn:

Cross-hatching

Your turn:

Squiggling

Your turn:

Pencil power!
Now use your new shading skills to give Mr. Mot's wildest shirt lots of "color"—using just a pen or pencil. I've done one shape already.

ME, ONLY OLDER

I cut out some magazine photos and drew some pictures to show what I hope the rest of my future life will be like.

DEAR ME!

Here's a letter I wrote to my future self. It's the now-me telling the older-me what I hope I'm doing and what life is like.

Dear Future Me, a.k.a. _____ (age ____),

_____

_____

_____

_____

_____

_____

_____

_____

Love,

_____ (age ____)

FROM ONE
ART-O-BIOGRAPHER
TO ANOTHER...CONGRATULATIONS!
YOUR BOOK IS <u>ALMOST AS</u>
COOL AS MINE ARE.

SINCE WE'RE BOOK BUDDIES NOW, YOU
MIGHT WANT TO JOIN MY FAN CLUB.
GO TO WWW.ALDOZELNICK.COM
AND CLICK ON THIS FLAG-THINGY!

SIGN UP TO RECEIVE:

- sneak preview chapters from my next book.
- an early look at coming book titles, covers, and more.
- opportunities to vote on new character names and other stuff.
- discounts on the books and merchandise.
- a card from me on your birthday (for kids)!

The Aldo Zelnick fan club is free and easy.
If you're under 13, ask your mom or dad to sign you up!